Fifty Shades of Coq

A PARODY COOKBOOK FOR LOVERS OF
WHITE COQ, DARK COQ,
AND ALL SHADES BETWEEN

EDITION 1

BY

A. F. OWLPUN

SAN FRANCISCO

Legal Notice

First Published 2015
Copyright Edition 1 © 2015

All rights reserved.

ISBN-13: 978-1515142027
ISBN-10: 1515142027

Foreplay

I know what you want. You bought this book because you're tired of forking the same old meat — stringy steak, fatty pork, boring burger.

Deep inside, you feel a new direction throbbing... you want to grab hold of something big and exciting, and take it in. You probably even fantasize about the thrill of handling a new coq — beating it to submission (more please!), binding it with rope (tighter mistress!), and guiding it into your quivering-hot oven. You clearly look forward to putting a perfectly tender, exotically seasoned, succulent piece of meat into your mouth, and enjoying its exotic flavors again and again. Admit it, you want to fork some coq!

You're in luck. This cookbook is the answer to all of your coq fantasies.

Here you will find coq in all its glory — main course, side meat, steamy stew, coq sliders, coq that's been beaten until tender, stuffed coq, white meat and dark. Maybe you have a fetish — you secretly love coq in your pie, or you crave coq sauce so savory it'll have you sucking bones. It's all here in 50 shades.

A warning: some recipes are not for the faint of heart. You'll find spicy, exotic, unknown pleasures. Maybe these recipes seem a little extreme, but how will you know until you try them? If things get too hot, you and your coq can always agree on a safe word.

So, what are you waiting for? Stop choking your chicken, go find a coq, lock yourself in your playroom and let yourself go!

Table of Contents

Coq Teasers

SALADS AND APPETIZERS

ARANCINI- ITALIAN CHICKEN & RICE CROQUETTES

Servings: About 2 dozen | Prep time: 20 minutes,

plus 20 to cook the rice | Cooking time: 20 minutes

Coq & balls—deep fried! Ouch! Handle gently, and turn the heat up for best results.

Ingredients:

4 cups Arborio rice

1 tablespoon olive oil

3 to 4 cloves garlic, minced

5 large eggs

1 1/2 cups Parmigiano-Reggiano cheese, grated

1 1/2 cups Italian-style breadcrumbs

2/3 cup chopped parsley

Kosher salt and freshly ground pepper

1 pound buffalo mozzarella cheese, cut into 1/2-inch cubes

1/2 pound thinly sliced prosciutto, cut into bite-sized pieces

Canola oil for frying

9

Directions:

1. Cook rice by directions and transfer to a large bowl; set aside until completely cooled.

2. While the rice is cooking , heat olive oil in a small skillet over medium-high heat. Add garlic and cook, stirring, about 2 minutes. Remove from heat and set aside.

3. Beat 3 eggs one at a time and stir them into the cooled rice. Add parmesan, parsley, and cooked garlic; stir to combine. Season with salt and pepper.

4. With wet hands, form rice mixture into a 2 1/2-inch balls and place them on a baking sheet. Make a thumbprint in each ball and fill it with 1 cube of mozzarella cheese and 1 piece of prosciutto. Press together to close like a purse, adding a bit more rice mixture to cover if needed.

5. Beat the remaining 2 eggs.

6. Scatter breadcrumbs on a wide plate. Dip each rice ball in egg mixture, then roll it in the breadcrumbs. Place the balls back on the baking sheet as you work.

7. Heat 5 inches of oil in pot until it reaches 350 degrees.

8. Place one rice ball at a time with a slotted spoon in the oil, and cook for 2-3 minutes. Transfer to a paper towel-covered plate. Serve with marinara sauce.

Chicken & Rice Noodle Salad

Servings: 4 | Prep time: 20 minutes | Cooking time: 30 minutes

These well-fondled breasts are at their best lathered up with sauce and just a little spice. When they get naughty, give them fifty lashes with a wet noodle.

Ingredients:

1 1/4 pounds boneless, skinless chicken breasts, shredded

Dressing

4 thinly sliced scallion whites

2 minced garlic cloves

1/2 cup soy sauce

1/2 cup rice vinegar

2 tablespoons light-brown sugar

1 tablespoon fresh lime juice

1/2 teaspoon red-pepper flakes

Kosher salt

3 1/2 ounces Chinese rice noodles

1 tablespoon vegetable oil

2 carrots, shredded

11

1 cucumber, peeled and thinly sliced

1/4 cup fresh basil, torn

Chopped peanuts

Directions:

1. Combine dressing ingredients and divide in half, one half to marinate the chicken for 30 minutes or overnight, one half to serve over the salad.

2. Cook noodles until tender in a large pot of boiling salted water, then drain them and transfer to your serving platter or plates.

3. Heat oil over medium-high heat in a large skillet. Working in batches, fry the chicken until cooked through, 1 to 2 minutes, placing cooked pieces on top of the noodles.

4. Drizzle with dressing and top with carrots, cucumber, basil, and peanuts.

CHICKEN & FARRO SALAD

Servings: About 2 dozen | Prep time: 20 minutes,

including 30 minutes to marinate | Cooking time: 1

hour

Are you a leg-man or -woman? Here are some trim, tart thighs marinated for succulent flavor. Toss them on the bed. . . of farro, that is.

Ingredients:

4 skinned and boned chicken thighs

Lemon Vinaigrette, divided

1 cup farro

2 1/4 teaspoons kosher salt, divided

2 garlic cloves

2 tablespoons olive oil

1/2 red onion, thinly sliced

1 fennel bulb, thinly sliced

10 sweet mini peppers, halved and seeded

1/2 cup loosely packed fresh parsley

1/3 cup basil leaves, torn

1 tablespoon fresh thyme

Directions:

1. Place chicken and 1/4 cup Lemon Vinaigrette in a 1-gallon resealable plastic bag. Seal and marinate for at least 30 minutes. (Reserve and chill remaining vinaigrette.)

2. Meanwhile, cook farro according to package directions with 1 teaspoon salt and the garlic cloves. Drain and rinse; discard garlic, and transfer farro to a large bowl.

3. Toss with onions, fennel and peppers. Add reserved lemon vinaigrette.

4. Sauté the marinated thighs in olive oil over medium heat in a large skillet. Serve them over the farrow and vegetables, sprinkled with parsley, basil, and thyme.

CHICKEN GYOZA

Servings: About 3 dozen gyoza | Prep time: 45 minutes | Cooking time: 45 minutes

The key to this recipe is to moisten the edges of the gyoza and give them a little pinch so they stay nice and tight. Don't you want a tight fit for that coq?

Ingredients:

Sauce:

1/2 cup soy sauce

1 teaspoon rice vinegar

1/2 teaspoon toasted sesame oil

2 teaspoons sugar

1 whole scallion, chopped fine

1 hot green chili, chopped fine

2 tablespoons water

Dumplings:

1/2 pound ground chicken

2 tablespoons peanut oil

1 cup bok choy, finely chopped

1/2 teaspoon fresh ginger, minced

1 garlic clove, minced

1 teaspoon soy sauce

1/2 teaspoon sesame oil

1/2 teaspoon coarse salt

1 large egg white

36 dumpling wrappers

Peanut oil, for frying

Directions:

1. Combine all the sauce ingredients and set aside.

2. Mix together the chicken, oil, bok choy, ginger, garlic, soy sauce, sesame oil, salt and egg white.

3. Spread dumpling wrappers on a work surface.

4. Spoon 1 teaspoon of filling into the center of each wrapper. Moisten the wrappers' edges with water and fold the dough over. Pinch to close. Place the dumplings on a baking sheet and keep them covered to prevent drying out as you work.

5. Heat a large skillet with about 1/4 to 1/2 inch of peanut oil. Add a single layer of gyoza. Cook them for 2 to 3 minutes, then left the edge to see if they're golden brown on the bottom, but don't turn them.

6.   Add 1/4 cup of water to the pan and cook, covered, 5 minutes, or until the meat is cooked through and the dumplings become unstuck from the bottom. Serve immediately with small bowls of sauce.

CHICKEN LIVER PÂTÉ

Servings: 2 1/2 cups | Prep time: 15 minutes |

Cooking time: 15 minutes

You know what pâté is, right? Chicken livers for chicken lovers. Don't be chicken. It's not hard to make. Just heat it, beat it, and spread it all over.

Ingredients:

1 tablespoon butter

2 tablespoons olive oil

1 medium yellow onion, diced

1 large carrot, grated

1 teaspoon fresh thyme

1/8 teaspoon cayenne pepper

Coarse salt and ground pepper

1 pound chicken livers, rinsed and trimmed of fat

Directions:

1. Heat 1 1/2 teaspoons butter and 1 tablespoon oil over medium heat in a large skillet.

2. Add onion and sauté thoroughly, about 10 minutes. Add carrot, thyme, and cayenne and season with salt and pepper. Cook until

carrot is tender, 5 minutes, stirring to prevent sticking. Transfer to a food processor.

3. To the same skillet, add remaining butter and oil. Gently dry livers with paper towels and season them with salt and pepper. Sauté until golden brown and cooked through, 5 minutes or a little more.

4. Transfer livers to the food processor and pulse until the mixture is smooth (it won't be completely without a few lumps and pieces, which add character). Season to taste with salt and pepper and let cool to room temperature.

CHICKEN SATAY SLIDERS

Servings: 8 | Prep time: 15 minutes | Cooking time: 15 minutes

You'll like this recipe if you're into things that slide down your throat. Each slider is juicy and just a little too big for a mouthful. Expect to get a little messy from the sticky, sloppy sauce!

Ingredients:

SAUCE:

1/2 cup chunky peanut butter

1/4 cup apple juice

3 tablespoons soy sauce

1 tablespoon Asian chili-garlic sauce or Sriracha

SLIDERS:

1 1/2 pounds ground turkey or chicken

2 scallions, or one tablespoon grated onion

2 cloves garlic, minced

1 piece (1 1/2 inches) fresh ginger, grated or finely chopped

Salt and pepper

1/4 cup vegetable oil

8 slider-size sandwich buns

TOPPINGS:

Shredded cabbage,

Chopped mint or cilantro

Directions:

1. Preheat grill to medium-high. Heat the peanut butter to soften— 30 seconds in the microwave, or in a pan on the stove over very low heat.

2. Add the juice, soy sauce, and chili sauce and combine thoroughly.

3. Combine the meat with the scallions or onions, garlic, ginger and oil, then season with salt and pepper. Form into 8 patties.

4. Grill 6-8 minutes, turning once, until cooked through. Serve the patties on slider buns, with lots of satay sauce and a sprinkling of cabbage and mint or cilantro.

CHICKEN-STRAWBERRY PIZZA WITH MINT AND BASIL

Servings: 4 | Prep time: 15 minutes | Cooking time:

10 minutes

True, this recipe isn't spicy or wild, but it's so unusual it could awaken your secret fetishist, whether you crave pizza, strawberries or coq.

Ingredients:

1½ oz. fresh mint leaves, coarsely chopped

1½ oz. fresh basil leaves, coarsely chopped

1 clove garlic, minced

Kosher salt

Juice of 1 lemon

1 tablespoon olive oil

1 lb. boneless, skinless chicken breast

4 individual prepared pizza crusts

½ lb. fresh strawberries, sliced

1/2 cup goat cheese

Directions:

1. Preheat oven to 425 degrees and prepare a barbecue grill.

2. Combine the mint, basil, garlic, salt, lemon juice and olive oil in a food processor and puree until it forms a paste like pesto.

3. Grill the chicken for about 4 minutes per side, then remove it and chop into cubes.

4. Place the pizza crusts on a baking sheet and bake for about 3-5 minutes.

5. Remove from the oven and spread with mint pesto. Sprinkle the chicken breast pieces onto of that, then spread the strawberries over the chicken. Top with goat cheese. Bake until the cheese melts.

CITRUS-SCENTED CHICKEN LIVERS

Servings: About 2 dozen | Prep time: 5 minutes |

Cooking time: 10 minutes

If you haven't tried chicken livers, this recipe is a great way to pop your cherry. Ardent fans praise their creaminess. Here they get just a little tart and zesty with a squeeze of lemon.

Ingredients:

1 pound chicken livers -rinsed and trimmed of fat

2 tablespoons olive oil

4 cloves garlic, minced

1 tablespoon lemon juice

1 tablespoon lemon zest

1/2 teaspoon salt, or to taste

Directions:

1. Gently dry chicken livers with a paper towel.

2. Sauté the chicken livers in the oil over medium heat until cooked through, 3 to 5 minutes.

3. Add lemon juice, zest, garlic and salt to livers; gently stir until mixed, and sauté another 2 or three minutes.

Korean-Style Fried Chicken Balls

Servings: 2 | Prep time: 20 minutes | Cook time: 20 minutes

Chickens have balls? Not really, but these tender pieces of chicken breast quick-fried to retain their own juices. You can turn them over in the savory sauce or serve it on the side.

Ingredients:

Sauce:

2 tablespoons rice vinegar

1 teaspoon salt

1/2 teaspoon black pepper

1 tablespoon minced garlic

1/2 tablespoon minced ginger

1 tablespoon chopped green onion

2 tablespoons soy sauce

1/2 tablespoon sesame oil

1 tablespoons chili flakes, or less to taste

1 tablespoons gochujang sauce

3 tablespoons honey

Chicken:

1/2 pound chicken breast

1 cup cornstarch

Batter:

1/2 cup tempura batter

1/4 teaspoon salt

1/2 cup ice water

1 cup frying oil

Directions:

1. Combine all the sauce ingredients in a sauce pan over low heat and cook for about 5 minutes. Set aside.

2. Cut up the chicken breasts in bite-sized pieces and coat them with cornstarch in a large bowl or by shaking them in a bag.

3. Blend the tempura batter ingredients in large bowl.

4. In a wok or deep skillet, heat the oil over medium high until a drop of water sizzles in it.

5. Dip the chicken in the batter one piece at a time and fry in the oil for 3-5 minutes, watching carefully. Place the fried chicken on paper towels.

6. Once you've finished frying the chicken you can either toss it in a large bowl with the sauce or serve it with the sauce on the side.

MALFOUF- MEDITERRANEAN CHICKEN-STUFFED CABBAGE ROLLS

Servings: 4 | Prep time: 30 minutes | Cooking time: 1 hour

C'mon, admit it—you like your roll stuffed with coq. Well, if you didn't before, you will now. In this recipe, steam is the key. So stuff it, roll tight, get steamy and enjoy.

Ingredients:

1 head of cabbage 2 cups rice

1 lb. ground lamb

1 tablespoon cumin 1 teaspoon allspices 2 tablespoon salt, divided

1/4 cup vegetable oil

4 cloves of garlic minced 1/4 cup lemon juice

Directions:

1. Carefully peel away cabbage leaves one at a time, discarding the outer, torn leaves. Place them in a deep pot of boiling water and blanch for about 3 minutes. Set blanched leaves in a colander to drain.

29

2. In a large bowl, add rice, meat, cumin, allspices, 1 tablespoon salt, and vegetable oil. Mix altogether until well combined.

3. Using leaves that are approximately 6x6 inches, spread about one tablespoon of meat mixture into the center of each leaf and roll it up.

4. Squeeze the roll a bit to tighten it and get rid of excess water. Place each roll in a large pot, layering the rolls as you work until you've filled half the pot. Sprinkle the top of that layer with 2 cloves of minced garlic and 1 tablespoon of salt, then continue rolling and layering until you've used all the meat and cabbage.

5. Sprinkle the topmost layer with the rest of the garlic and salt.

6. Fill the pot with water until it just covers the rolls. Heat to boiling in the covered pot, then reduce the heat to simmer and cook for about 45 minutes.

7. Add half quantity of the chopped garlic. Continue to layer up the pot with cabbage rolls. Add the remaining amount of garlic, 1 tablespoon of salt, and cube of stock.

8.   Cover cabbage rolls by water (same level of the rolls) and place the pot over a medium heat until water is boiling. Cover the pot, reduce the heat to the minimum and let simmer for about 45 minutes until the rice is fully cooked. Add the lemon juice to the pot before serving.

Middle Eastern Chicken Hawashi

Servings: 6 | Prep time: 20 minutes | Cooking time: 25 minutes

Ever stuffed your meat into a warm pocket dripping with melted butter? Oh yes, you read right: this recipe gets hot, steamy, and kinky.

Ingredients:

1 pound (450 grams) of lean ground beef

1 onion, diced

1 roma tomato, diced

2 cloves garlic, mince

2 tablespoons fresh chopped parsley

2 tablespoons fresh chopped cilantro

1 green pepper, diced

1/2 teaspoon cayenne pepper

1/2 teaspoon cinnamon

Kosher salt to taste

6 pita bread pockets

1/4 cup butter, melted

Directions:

1. Preheat oven to 400 degrees

2. In a large bowl, combine all the ingredients but the pita bread and butter.

3. Stuff each pita pocket with an equal amount of the meat mixture, and brush the outside with melted butter.

4. Wrap each one in a piece of parchment paper or foil. If you're using foil, poke a small hole so moisture can escape.

5. Bake until the outside of the bread is crispy, about 20-25 minutes, and the meat is cooked through.

Spicy Chicken-Lettuce Wraps

Servings: 4 | Prep time: 20 minutes | Cook time: 10 minutes

An alternative to tossing your salad. Try this spicy number, featuring (chicken) breasts redolent with dark oil and spicy flavors.

Ingredients:

2 1/2 ounces bean noodles

1/4 cup fresh cilantro

1/4 cup soy sauce

1 tablespoon chili paste

2 cloves garlic, minced

2 teaspoons dark sesame oil

2 cups roasted skinless, boneless chicken breast, shredded

12 large Boston or Romaine lettuce leaves

Directions:

1. Pour boiling water over the bean threads and let them stand until softened, about 5 minutes. Drain them and chop into bite-sized pieces.

2. While bean threads are soaking, combine cilantro, soy sauce, chili paste, garlic, and oil in a large bowl.

3. Add noodles and chicken and toss well to coat. Spoon about 1/3 cup chicken mixture down center of each lettuce leaf to serve.

STUFFED CHICKEN & ZUCCHINI SALAD

Servings: 24 pieces | Prep time: 10 minutes |

Cooking time: 20 minutes

If you like your zucchini long, hard and ready to burst, you'll love this recipe. Keep the jalapeños to a minimum if your tastes run mild.

Ingredients

1½ lbs. zucchini

1 1/2 cups cooked chicken breast

2 tablespoons cream cheese

½ cup shredded cheese

¼ cup pickled jalapenos, chopped (for more spice, add more jalapenos)

Directions:

---

1. Preheat oven to 350 degrees and prepare a baking sheet with parchment paper or oil.

2. Cut zucchini in half longways and scoop out the seeds.

3. Combine chicken, cream cheese, ¼ cup of grated cheese, and jalapeños in a large bowl.

4.   Fill each zucchini with an equal amount of the chicken-cheese mixture, then sprinkle with remaining cheese.

5.   Bake for 20 minutes or until the cheeses are bubbly.

Fetishes

ROLLED, STUFFED AND TRUSSED-UP

CHICKEN CANNELLONI

Servings: 4 | Prep time: 25 minutes | Cooking time:

30 minutes

Julia Child, one of history's most famous coq-handlers, is said to have exclaimed of cannelloni, "These damn things are as hot as a stiff cock." How can steamy tubes of meat and sauce be anything but?

Ingredients:

Cannelloni Filling:

8 ounces cooked chicken breast, cubed

1 cup fresh spinach, chopped

1/4 cup sun-dried tomatoes, roughly chopped

2 cups ricotta cheese

1/2 cup mozzarella cheese, shredded

1/2 teaspoon black pepper

1 teaspoon salt

12 cooked lasagna noodles

Cannelloni Sauce:

2 cups Alfredo sauce

2 cups marinara sauce

1/2 cup Parmesan cheese, grated

Directions:

1. Preheat oven to 350 degrees.

2. Make the Filling: In a large bowl, combine chicken, spinach, tomatoes, ricotta, mozzarella, pepper and salt, and mix thoroughly.

3. Make the Cannelloni: Arrange the lasagna noodles on a flat surface and place about a quarter cup of filling down the center of each pasta sheet. Roll the lasagna around the mixture, and place in a baking dish.

4. Combine Alfredo sauce and tomato sauce in bowl. Pour the sauce over rolled cannelloni. Sprinkle grated Parmesan cheese, cover with foil and bake at for 20 minutes. Remove foil and continue to bake for an additional 10-15 minutes.

CHICKEN KIEV

Servings: 4 | Prep time: 35 minutes, plus 2 hours of

cooling time | Cooking time: 10 minutes

Paddle this coq firmly, roll it up, then heat until it nearly pops. Apparently that's how they do it in Kiev.

Ingredients:

1 stick butter, room temperature

1 teaspoon dried parsley

1 teaspoon dried tarragon

Salt and pepper to taste

4 boneless, skinless chicken breast halves

2 large whole eggs

2 1/4 cups Panko

Vegetable oil, for frying

Directions:

1. In the bowl of a mixer, combine butter, parsley, tarragon, about a teaspoon of salt and pepper to taste and beat until thoroughly mixed.

2. Place this compound butter onto a sheet of plastic wrap, roll into a log shape and put it in the freezer. When its consistency is that

of refrigerated butter, cut it into four equal pieces.

3.   Beat the chicken breast between plastic wrap or wax paper until they're 1/4 to 1/8 an inch thick. Season with salt and pepper.

4.   Place 1/4 of the compound butter and 1 tablespoon of Panko in the center of each flattened chicken breast.

5.   Roll breast into a tight log, completely enclosing the butter and tucking in the ends. Repeat with each breast. Refrigerator rolled chicken for 2 hours, or as long as overnight.

6.   Beat eggs and pour them into a pie plate or shallow bowl. Scatter the Panko onto another pie plate or shallow bowl.

7.   Heat 1/2-inch of vegetable oil to 375 degrees in a skillet or sauce pan over medium-high heat.

8.   Coat each breast in beaten egg and roll in the bread crumbs.

9.   Gently place each breast in the skillet edge side first, and cook 4 to 5 minutes on each side, until the internal temperature reaches 165 degrees F.

10.   Remove rolls to a cooling rack set over a baking pan and allow to drain for 5 to 10 minutes before serving.

CHICKEN ROULADE

Servings: 6 | Prep time: 35 minutes | Cooking time:

35 minutes

Here's a recipe where you can take your coq in hand and beat it. Keep restraints taut but not so tight as to leave any marks on the delicate flesh.

Ingredients:

1 cup fine breadcrumbs

1 1/2 cups chopped almonds, divided

2 teaspoons extra-virgin olive oil

6 cloves of garlic, minced

2 shallots, finely chopped, or 2 tablespoons grated onion

3 cups mushrooms

1 tablespoon fresh thyme

1/2 cup spinach

1 tablespoon water

3 boneless, skinless chicken breast halves

Salt and pepper to taste.

Directions:

1.   Preheat oven to 375 degrees.

2. Pulse 3/4 cup almonds in a food processor until finely ground and blend with the breadcrumbs.

3. Over medium heat, cook garlic and shallots in oil until soft, about 4 minutes.

4. Add the mushrooms and thyme, and sauté until mushrooms are slightly golden, about 4 minutes; remove from heat, and set aside.

5. In the same pan, add spinach and water and cook until just wilted, about a minute. Drain the spinach, chop it, and combine it with the mushroom mixture. Stir in remaining almonds.

6. Butterfly the chicken breasts, and beat them between plastic wrap or wax paper until they're 1/4 to 1/8 an inch thick.

7. Season with salt and pepper. Lay 1 chicken breast on your work surface and spread 1/2 cup mushroom-walnut mixture down its center, with a 1/2-inch border on all sides.

8. Roll the breast and tie with kitchen twine. Cover the roll with crumbs and almonds, pressing to coat.

9. Transfer to a baking sheet and bake for about 25 minutes, until a thermometer inserted into the center reads 165 degrees. Remove the twine and slice into inch wide pieces.

CHICKEN STUFFED WITH MAPLE BACON

Servings: 4 | Prep time: 10 minutes | Cooking time:

50 minutes

Do you like to get porked, or do you prefer to do the porking? Either way, this recipe is a great way to enjoy coq. Stuff it with the greasy pork goodness of bacon and get ready to wipe a lot of, uh, juices off your chin.

Ingredients:

4 boneless, skinless chicken breasts

4 slices maple-flavored bacon, cooked and crumbled

1/2 cup goat cheese

1/2 teaspoon salt

1/4 teaspoon pepper

1 tablespoon olive oil

1 teaspoon cornstarch

2/3 cup chicken broth

2 tablespoons parsley finely chopped

Directions:

1. Preheat the oven to 375 degrees and oil an oven-proof skillet.

2. Cut a pocket about an inch deep and an inch wide into the thickest side of each chicken breast.

3. Stuff each half with equal amounts of the cheese and bacon. Seal with a toothpick.

4. Transfer to a baking sheet and bake for about 30-40 minutes, until a thermometer inserted into the center reads 165 degrees.

5. Remove the chicken breasts to a platter or individual plates.

6. Place the skillet over medium high heat and add the chicken broth. Whisk in the cornstarch thoroughly, getting rid of any lumps. Bring this mixture to a boil as you stir and scrape the bits of cooked chicken from the pan.

7. Continue to cook until reduced by half and serve with the chicken, a sprinkling of parsley as the final touch.

CRANBERRY-STUFFED, PROSCIUTTO-WRAPPED CHICKEN

Servings: just 2 romantic servings | Prep time: 35 minutes | Cooking time: 30 minutes

For those who enjoy beating their meat... Start with a firm paddling, wrap it tight, then tie it up like a gimp. It's a recipe you're, ahem, *bound* to enjoy.

Ingredients:

1 tablespoon olive oil

1/3 cup dried cranberries, chopped

1/4 cup plain bread crumbs

1 egg yolk

1 1/2 tablespoons finely grated parmesan cheese

2 teaspoons olive oil 1 teaspoon fresh thyme

1 teaspoon fresh oregano, minced

2 cloves garlic, minced

salt and pepper to taste

Pinch cayenne pepper

2 (6 ounce) skinless, boneless chicken breast halves

4 thin slices prosciutto 3/4 cup chicken broth

1 1/2 tablespoons balsamic vinegar

1 tablespoon butter salt and pepper to taste

Directions:

1. Preheat the oven to 400 degrees F and oil an ovenproof skillet.

2. Combine cranberries, bread crumbs, egg yolk, cheese, olive oil, thyme, oregano, garlic, salt, black pepper, and cayenne pepper.

3. Butterfly the chicken breasts, and beat them between plastic wrap or wax paper until they're 1/4 to 1/8 an inch thick. Season with salt and pepper.

4. Place half the stuffing on each breast and roll into a tight roll. It might help to roll up the breasts with a piece of plastic wrap and twist the ends to make the roll tight.

5. Lay out enough prosciutto to span the width of the chicken roll. Starting at one end, roll the chicken in the prosciutto.

6. On your work surface, lay out 4 pieces of string 1 -inch apart. Place chicken roll across the strings, and tie each strand around the roll.

7. Place the rolls in the skillet and bake them for about 25 minutes, until a thermometer inserted into the center reads 165 degrees.

8. To prepare the sauce, drain half the accumulated fat grease from the pan and

put the skillet over high heat on the stove. Add chicken stock and balsamic vinegar, and bring to a boil. Boil while scraping the pan and stirring, until liquid has reduced by half, 5 to 6 minutes. Add the butter and remove from heat. Season with salt and pepper to taste, but be aware the sauce will already be pretty salty.

9. Cut the strings from chicken rolls and slice them into inch-thick pieces. Serve drizzled with sauce.

When You're Hot, You're Hot

SAUTÉED, ROASTED, BROILED, BRAISED AND
BAKED

ALMOND-POMEGRANATE CHICKEN

Servings: 4 | Prep time: 10 minutes | Cooking time:10 minutes

The grill leaves little love-bite marks on this coq. Plus, almonds, honey and pomegranate are all potent aphrodisiacs. Serve this for dinner and retire to the playroom for the rest of the evening!

Ingredients:

Juice of 1 lemon

1/4 cup honey

1/3 cup pomegranate juice

1/2 cup olive oil

2 tablespoons orange juice

2 tablespoons lime juice

1/2 tablespoon rosemary

4 chicken breasts

1 cup almonds, chopped

Directions:

1. Combine all ingredients up to the chicken in a re-sealable plastic freezer bag. Add the chicken and turn to coat. Refrigerate overnight or for at least 2 hours.

2.   Prepare grill. Grill chicken and serve topped with almonds.

CHICKEN ADOBO

Servings: 4 | Prep time: 10 minutes plus time to marinate (2-24 hours) | Cooking time:1 hour, 10 minutes

Who doesn't like hot thighs dripping with cream? If that sounds a little "vanilla", add some Thai chili to heat things up.

Ingredients:

1 cup coconut milk

¼ cup soy sauce

1½ cup rice vinegar

12 garlic cloves, peeled

2-3 whole Thai chilis

3 bay leaves

1½ teaspoons freshly ground black pepper

3 to 4 pounds chicken thighs

Directions:

1. Combine all ingredients up to the chicken in a resealable plastic freezer bag. Add the chicken and turn to coat. Refrigerate overnight or for at least 2 hours.

2. Preheat the oven to broil.

3.   Bring the chicken and marinade to a boil over high heat in a large lidded pot over high heat. Reduce to a simmer and cook, stirring occasionally, about 30 minutes, until the chicken is cooked through.

4.   Remove the chicken from the pot, increase the heat and simmer the sauce about 10 minutes. Remove bay leaves and chilies.

5.   Place the chicken under the broiler on a roasting pan and place under broiler for 5 to 7 minutes, then baste with the sauce. Let the chicken cook for another five minutes, baste again, and cook for 3-5 minutes more.

6.   Remove the chicken from the oven, return it to the sauce pot, and serve, either in the pot itself or in a platter, covered with sauce.

CHICKEN CHASSEUR

Servings: 4 | Prep time: 20 minutes | Cooking time: 25 minutes

Are you the hunter or the hunted in this coq fantasy? You might need to play both roles to figure out which you like best. Enjoy this rustic dish hot off the stove, or try it leftover (if you're into sloppy seconds).

Ingredients:

1/2 ounce dried porcini mushrooms

1 1/2 cups chicken stock

1 1/2 pounds chicken breast cutlets, cut into large pieces

Salt and pepper

Flour, for dredging

2 tablespoons olive oil

4 tablespoons butter, divided

2 carrots, peeled and finely chopped

2 large shallots, finely chopped

2 large cloves garlic, finely chopped

1/4 cup brandy

1/2 cup dry white wine

1 can diced tomatoes (14.5 ounces)

3 tablespoons fresh tarragon, chopped

8 ounces extra-wide egg noodles

Directions:

1. Heat the chicken stock to a simmer in a small pan and add the mushrooms. Remove from heat and set aside.

2. Bring a medium pot of water to a boil.

3. Salt and pepper the chicken thoroughly and dredge in flour.

4. Heat the olive oil in a large skillet over medium-high. Add the chicken and sauté until brown on both sides and cooked through, 3-5 minutes; set it aside.

5. Reducing the heat to medium, add 3 tablespoons of butter to the skillet and sauté the carrots, shallots and garlic. Season with salt and pepper. Cook until the vegetables are softened, 3-5 minutes.

6. Add the brandy to the hot pan, scraping to loosen any cooked bits, then stir in the wine. Drain the mushrooms, chop them and them and the stock they cooked in to the pan. Add the tomatoes and tarragon. Finally, add the chicken and simmer about 10 minutes.

CHICKEN MOGLAI

Servings: 8 | Prep time: 30 minutes | Cooking time:

20 minutes

If you've had enough of everyday loving, try this recipe for a night of complete abandon. Here, you have a chance to seriously warm things up by blending your own spice mix. Might be a good idea to agree on a safe-word.

Ingredients:

1 1-inch piece ginger

4 cloves garlic

2 teaspoons ground cumin

1 teaspoon ground coriander

1/2 teaspoon dried chili flakes

4 tablespoons ground almonds

1/2 cup water

Seeds of 5 cardamom pods

1 cinnamon stick

2 bay leaves

1/4 cup vegetable oil

3 pounds boned chicken thighs cut in half

2 onions, finely chopped

1 cup Greek yogurt

1 cup chicken stock

1/2 cup heavy cream

1/2 cup raisins (golden raisins are traditional for this dish, but any will do)

1 teaspoon garam masala

1 tablespoon sugar

1 teaspoon salt

3/4 cup toasted, flaked almonds

Directions:

1. Put the ginger, garlic, cumin, coriander, and chili into a food processor, or into a mortar and pestle, and pulse or crush until thoroughly combines. Add the ground almonds and water and then blend to a paste. Set aside.

2. Heat the oil in a large pan over medium-high and add the chicken pieces and fry them in batches until they are just brown on the outside.

3. Remove the chicken and add the spice paste and onions to the oil and stir to combine thoroughly. Add the yogurt, about a third at a time, blending it thoroughly with the oil, then stir in the stock, cream, and raisins.

4. Return the browned chicken and its juices to the pan, and sprinkle the garam masala, sugar, and salt. Cover and cook on a medium-low for 25 minutes. Serve topped with toasted almonds.

Chicken Manchurian

Servings: 4 | Prep time: 20 minutes | Cooking time:

35 minutes

This recipe will make your coq tart and sassy. Remember — don't touch your eyes, or any other sensitive body parts, after handling jalapeño. Some excitements are better off left in the fantasy realm.

Ingredients:

---

1 lb. boneless, skinless chicken breasts, cut into bite-sized pieces

1/2 - 1 cup vegetable oil for frying

Batter:

2 Egg whites

2 tablespoon cornstarch

2 tablespoon flour

Salt and pepper to taste

1 teaspoon white wine vinegar

1 1/2 teaspoons soy sauce

1 1/2 teaspoon red chili sauce

Sauce:

1 tablespoon grated ginger

3 cloves garlic, crushed

1/2 jalapeño, seeded and chopped

2 1/2 cups chicken stock

1 1/2 cups water

2 tablespoons soy sauce

2 tablespoons ketchup

1 1/2 tablespoons red chili sauce, like Sriracha

1 teaspoon white wine vinegar

1/2 teaspoon sugar

Salt to taste

1 1/5 tablespoons cornstarch

3 scallions, chopped

Oil for frying

Directions:

1. Combine all batter ingredients and thoroughly coat the chicken. Heat the oil over medium-high and add chicken pieces, frying them in batches.

2. Remove fried chicken to a plate. Pour off most of the oil, leaving just enough to sauté the ginger and garlic.

3.   Add jalapeños, chicken stock and all the other ingredients of the sauce up to the cornstarch. Cook for 2-3 minutes, then whisk in the cornstarch thoroughly and bring to a gentle boil.

4.   Add fried chicken pieces and cook for 2-3 minutes. Serve garnished with scallions.

CHICKEN NANBANZUKE

Servings: 2 | Prep time: 15 minutes | Cooking time:

30 minutes

Here's how chicken gets sexy in Japan: Make it wet, add spicy excitement, then heat those thighs until they quiver. When you're spent from pleasure, lie back and lick the delicious memories off your lips.

Ingredients:

Sauce:

1/2 cup rice vinegar

1/2 cup mirin

1/4 cup soy sauce

4 tablespoons sugar

1 piece dried kombu seaweed

1 tablespoon Worcestershire sauce

2-3 small red Thai red chili peppers, chopped

1/2 teaspoon salt

Chicken:

5 chicken thighs

Vegetable oil for deep frying

3/4 cup cornstarch

1 Chinese eggplant

1 red bell pepper

1 yellow bell pepper

Directions:

1. Combine all sauce ingredients in a large bowl. Cut chicken into bite-sized pieces. Add chicken and coat thoroughly. Dice eggplant and peppers.

2. In a large skillet, heat ½ inch of oil over medium high heat. Scatter corn starch in a shallow bowl or plate. When oil is hot, dredge the eggplant and peppers in corn starch and shake to remove excess.

3. Deep fry the eggplant and peppers, working in batches and leaving plenty of room around each item, until golden brown. Transfer it to a wire rack or a paper towel.

4. Remove the chicken from marinade. Pour marinade into a non-reactive pan and bring to a boil. Boil 1 minute, then reduce heat and simmer for 3-5 minutes, and remove from heat.

5. Finally, dredge and fry the chicken. Serve chicken and vegetables with sauce.

CHICKEN PICCATA

Servings: 2 | Prep time: 15 minutes | Cooking time: 15 minutes

In our house "Piccata" means wild and crazy. For a more obedient coq, try a hard spanking between sheets of wax paper.

Ingredients:

2 boneless, skinless chicken breasts

Kosher salt and black pepper to taste

1/2 cup flour

1 egg

3/4 cup breadcrumbs

Olive oil

3 tablespoons butter, room temperature, divided

2 lemons

1/2 cup dry white wine

2 tablespoons capers

Sliced lemon, for serving

Chopped fresh parsley leaves, for serving

Directions:

1. Preheat the oven to 400 degrees and oil a baking dish.

2. Butterfly the chicken breasts, and beat them between plastic wrap or wax paper until they're 1/4 to 1/8 an inch thick. Sprinkle both sides with salt and pepper.

3. On a shallow dish or plate, combine the flour, 1/2 teaspoon salt, and 1/4 teaspoon of pepper.

4. Thoroughly beat the egg and pour it into a second shallow dish or plate. On a third plate, place the bread crumbs. Dredge each breast in the flour, shaking to remove excess, and then dip in the egg and bread crumbs.

5. In a large sauté pan over medium to medium-low heat, heat 1 tablespoon of olive oil. Sauté the chicken breasts and cook for 2 minutes on each side. Place them on the baking dish and cook in the oven for 5-10 minutes.

6. Meanwhile, in the same pan, melt 1 tablespoon of the butter, then add the juice of both lemons and their squeezed out peels, capers, and salt and pepper. Bring to a boil over high heat and cook, stirring and scraping, until reduced by half, just a couple of minutes. Remove from heat and add 2 tablespoons of butter.

7.   Discard the lemon peels and serve chicken
      breasts topped with sauce.

CHICKEN & WATERMELON RIND STIR-FRY

Servings: 4 | Prep time: 15 minutes | Cooking time: 15 minutes

Watermelon rind is considered a serious male aphrodisiac. Get ready for some thumpin'!

Ingredients:

1 1/2 pounds boneless, skinless chicken breasts, cut into bite-sized pieces

Salt and pepper to taste

3 tablespoons peanut oil, divided

1 onion, thinly sliced 3 cloves garlic, minced

1 teaspoon salt

1 cup peeled and sliced watermelon rind

1 red bell pepper, sliced thin

1 cup vegetable broth, divided

1/4 cup teriyaki sauce 2 tablespoons cornstarch

Directions:

1. Season the chicken pieces with salt and pepper and sauté them in 1 1/2 tablespoons peanut oil. Remove and set aside.

2. Add the rest of the ingredients up to the vegetable broth to the same pan with the remaining peanut oil and sauté for about 5 minutes.

3. Add the vegetable broth, reserving 2 tablespoons, and bring the mixture to a simmer for 5 minutes.

4. In a small bowl, whisk together the 2 tablespoons of broth and the cornstarch, then add this mixture to the pan with the teriyaki sauce.

5. Simmer a few minutes more and serve.

CHICKEN PAILLARDS

Servings: 2 | Prep time: 10 minutes | Cooking time:

10 minutes

Whether you like to choke your chicken or spank it into submission, this recipe serves up some delicious coq. A thorough beating results in tender, compliant chicken that gets warm and slick with both olive oil and butter. That's slippery coq!

Ingredients:

2 boneless, skinless chicken breast halves, tenders removed

Salt and pepper to taste

1 tablespoon olive oil

1 tablespoon butter

Directions:

1. Butterfly the chicken breasts, and beat them between plastic wrap or wax paper until they're 1/4 to 1/8 an inch thick. Sprinkle both sides with salt and pepper.

2. In a large skillet, heat olive oil and butter over medium-high heat until the butter gets foamy.

3. Add the chicken and sauté on one side until golden brown, about 2 minutes.

4. With the heat reduced to medium, turn the chicken and sauté another 2-3 minutes. Serve immediately.

CHICKEN TAGINE

Servings: 6 | Prep time: 10 minutes | Cooking time:

1 hour 20 minutes

A tagine is like a Moroccan crockpot (or in this case, a "coq-pot", wink wink). This recipe has a little of everything (including plenty of breasts, legs and thighs) and lots of coq-drippings to stir up the best flavors.

Ingredients:

3/4 cup dried apricots

2/3 cup orange juice

1 whole chicken cut into 10 pieces

Salt and pepper to taste

1 tablespoon olive oil

1 red onion, thinly sliced

2 cloves garlic, crushed

3 cups carrots, cut in thick rounds

1 1/2 teaspoons ground ginger

3/4 teaspoon ground cinnamon

2 cups chicken broth

3/4 cup raw almonds

1/2 cup green olives, pitted (no pimentos, though!)

Directions:

1. Over medium-high heat, bring apricots and orange juice to a simmer, then immediately remove and let cool.

2. Season chicken with salt and pepper. Heat a deep skillet over medium-high heat and cook the chicken in batches, until browned on all sides. Transfer to plate.

3. Pour off about half of the accumulated fat and reduce heat to medium.

4. Add onion, garlic, and carrots. Sauté the onion until it's translucent, about 3 minutes. Add ginger and cinnamon, stirring until fragrant, less than a minute.

5. Whisk in the broth and scrape browned bits from the bottom of the pan. Return chicken and its drippings to the pan.

6. Drain apricots and add them to pan along with the almonds and olives. Bring to a boil, then reduce to a simmer, partially covered, for 30-40 minutes, until a thermometer inserted in thickest part of chicken breast (without touching bone) reads 165 degrees.

Coq Au Vin

Servings: 6 | Prep time: 30 minutes | Cooking time:

2 hours— it's worth it

The French sure know their coq. Old school, sure, but sexy. They like to get their coq a little drunk (yes, that's a whole bottle of wine) in preparation for its big appearance.

Ingredients:

1 bottle light red wine, such as Beaujolais Nouveau

2 teaspoons fresh thyme

1 bay leaf

1/2 cup cooked, crumbled bacon

2 tablespoons olive oil

3 whole chicken legs

Salt and freshly ground pepper, to taste

1 lb. white mushrooms

1 cup shallots, halved

1 Tablespoon unsalted butter

3 garlic cloves, minced

2 tablespoons tomato paste

2 tablespoon flour

1 3/4 cups chicken broth

2 cups sliced carrots

Directions:

1. Preheat an oven to 350°F.

2. Boil the wine in a large, non-reactive pot until reduced by half, about 15 minutes.

3. In a heavy saucepan with a top, cook the bacon until crisp, 10 to 12 minutes.

4. Transfer to a paper towel-lined plate to drain. Discard all but 2 Tablespoons of the fat from the pot. Season the chicken with salt and pepper.

5. Set the pot over medium-high heat. Working in 2 batches, brown the chicken, turning once, 8 to 10 minutes per batch. Transfer to a plate.

6. Season the chicken with salt and pepper and sauté it over medium heat until it's golden brown on both sides.

7. Add the shallots and sauté for 5 minutes more. Transfer chicken and shallots to a plate. Return the pan to the heat, and add butter, garlic, tomato paste and flour and stir to combine.

8. Whisk in the reduced wine and the chicken broth, raise the heat to medium-high and simmer the sauce.

9. Add the bacon, chicken, mushroom, carrots, thyme and bay leaf. Cover, place in the

oven, and bake until the chicken is tender, about an hour and a half.

10. Remove the sauce pan from the oven and transfer the chicken to a plate.

11. Skim the fat off the drippings, set the pot over medium-high and simmer until it thickens, about 15 minutes.

12. Season with salt and pepper and serve.

PAPRIKA CHICKEN

Servings: 6 | Prep time: 15 minutes | Cooking time:

30 minutes

If you're a leg-man or -woman, you won't be able to restrain yourself from this dangerously yummy combination of subtle spice and chicken thighs. Remember to beat in the paprika thoroughly— that's the only way to get it to behave.

Ingredients:

8 chicken thighs, skin-on and bone-in

1 tablespoon olive oil

2 cups finely chopped onion

1/4 teaspoon salt

2 tablespoons paprika

1 (14-oz) can whole tomatoes, drained

1/2 cup chicken broth or water

1 1/2 teaspoons flour whisked with 1 tablespoon water

2 tablespoons sour cream, plus additional for serving

2 tablespoons chopped fresh parsley (optional)

Directions:

1. Remove skin and reserve. Pat chicken dry with paper towels.

2. Over medium heat, heat oil in a heavy pot then cook skin to render fat. Discard skin with a slotted spoon and add onion and salt, sautéing until onion is limp, about five minutes.

3. Whisk in paprika and cook for 1 minute. Stir in tomatoes and broth. Add chicken and simmer, covered, stirring occasionally, 10 minutes.

4. Remove the lid and continue cooking until chicken is just cooked through, not more than 10 minutes.

5. Stir flour and water mixture and whisk into sauce. Whisk and simmer until sauce is slightly thickened, about 2 minutes.

6. Remove from heat, add salt and whisk in sour cream. Serve with egg noodles, boiled potatoes, or rice.

SIMPLE SALT ROASTED CHICKEN

Servings: 4-6 | Prep time: 20 minutes | Cooking time: 1 hour

Nothing fancy, just an afternoon hot coq tied up and ready to enjoy.

Ingredients:

Simple Salt Roasted Chicken (mild)

1 roasting chicken

2 tablespoons Kosher salt

Juice of 1 lemon

Directions:

---

1. Heat oven to 450.

2. Douse the chicken with the lemon juice, then let it stand at room temperature for 15 minutes.

3. Pat off excess moisture with paper towels. Cover the chicken with salt, top, bottom, and inside out. Truss.

4.   Place the chicken on a roasting rack in a pan in the oven and roast, undisturbed, for up to one hour, until a thermometer inserted in the thigh shows at least 165 degrees. Remove the chicken from the oven and let stand 15 minutes before serving.

Spicy Chicken with Shrimp & Pepper Paste

Servings: 2 | Prep time: 15 minutes plus 1 hour and 15 minutes of standing time | Cooking time: 15 minutes

Here's an oral delight that will leave your lips tender and tingling with the memory of hot coq. Reduce the amount of red chilis if you can't handle the heat!

Ingredients:

6 dry red chilis, such as Thai

6 medium shallots, peeled and quartered

6 cloves garlic, peeled

1 1/2-inch piece ginger, chopped into large chunks

4 tablespoons vegetable oil, divided

Salt

1 pound boneless, skinless, chicken breast, cut into bite-sized pieces

12 ounces shrimp, peeled and deveined

1 teaspoon belachan, shrimp paste

2 teaspoons lime juice

1 teaspoon light brown sugar

Directions:

1. Cover the chilies in boiling water and let stand for 15 minutes before draining.

2. Place them in a food processor along with shallots, garlic, ginger, 2 tablespoons olive oil, and salt to taste (about 1 teaspoonful). Pulse to a coarse paste.

3. In a medium bowl, toss chicken and shrimp with 2 tablespoons chili paste. Cover and refrigerate for 1 hour.

4. Heat remaining oil in a wok or large nonstick skillet over medium-low heat.

5. Add remaining chili paste and the belachan and cook, stirring, about 5 minutes.

6. Add lime juice and sugar.

7. Increase the heat to medium high and add chicken.

8. Stir to combine, then add shrimp. Continue to cook another 3-5 minutes, until both chicken and shrimp are cooked through. Season to taste with salt. Serve with steamed rice.

Get It Wet

SOUPS, STEWS AND CURRIES

Avgolemono Soup

Servings: 4 | Prep time: 10 minutes | Cooking time: 35 minutes

Avgolemono is Greece's accidentally sexy soup: grains of orzo swimming in warm, eggy broth. Its secret pleasure — and surprisingly dark undertone — comes from the unlikely hookup of well whipped eggs and tart lemon. Serve with rice, or with a stiff crust of good baguette that softens when soaked.

Ingredients:

5 cups chicken broth

8 ounces boneless, skinless chicken breast

1/2 cup orzo

2 large eggs, lightly beaten

1/4 cup fresh lemon juice

Salt and pepper to taste

1/2 cup fresh dill, chopped

Prepare orzo according to package directions.

Directions:

1. Poach the chicken in the broth until it's thoroughly cooked through. Remove the chicken to a cutting board and let it cool

enough that you can shred it with your hands.

2. Add orzo and shredded chicken to broth remaining in the pot. Bring the mixture to a simmer, and reduce heat to low.

3. In a medium bowl, whisk together eggs and lemon juice until thoroughly combined.

4. Combine 1 cup hot broth with the egg and lemon mixture, whisking constantly, then stir this mixture back into the main pot.

5. Season with salt and pepper, and serve sprinkled with the dill.

BUTTER CHICKEN

Servings: 4 | Prep time: 15 minutes | Cooking time: 45 minutes

Brando said it best: Get the butter. Nothing else makes pleasure quite so rich and decadent. Here's buttery coq at its best, not just a gamey ol' rooster, but dense and toothsome (chicken) breasts, well-greased and laid out for your enjoyment.

Ingredients:

1/2 cup olive oil

1 1/2 lbs. boneless skinless chicken breasts

3 tablespoons butter

1 tablespoon garam masala

1 tablespoon lemon juice

1 tablespoon chili powder

1 cup yogurt

Salt to taste

6 garlic cloves

1 tablespoon chili powder

2 tablespoons ginger paste

1 tablespoon lemon juice

1 tablespoon olive oil

1 tablespoon butter

1 1⁄2 tablespoons garam masala

1 tablespoon ginger paste

1 tablespoon garlic paste

1 green chili pepper, diced

1 (28 ounce) can crushed tomatoes

1 tablespoon tomato paste

1 tablespoon chili powder

1⁄2 tablespoon honey or 1⁄2 tablespoon sugar

2 teaspoons dried fennel seeds

1 cup heavy cream

Directions:

1. Preheat oven to 400°F. Oil the chicken and bake it in the oven for 10 minutes; turn chicken and continue baking another 7-10 minutes.

2. In a large sauce pan over medium heat, melt butter and add garam masala. When masala scents, add ginger, garlic paste and green chili peppers. Sauté 5 minutes, then add crushed tomatoes, tomato paste, chili powder and salt to taste. Bring to a boil; reduce heat to low and simmer, and add honey, fennel seeds and cream.

3. Add the chicken to the sauce and simmer over very low heat until the sauce is reduced by half.

4. Serve with steamed rice.

CAJUN CHICKEN RAGOUT

Servings: 4 | Prep time: 25 minutes | Cooking time:

35 minutes

Oh, them Cajuns know how to cook so good it'll make you want to spank your momma. This recipe is full-up with all the salty, saucy, spicy delights Cajun cooking is famous for: Andouille, cayenne, bacon, and a rich and sticky roux. Is it good for you? Don't you think all intense pleasures are?

Ingredients:

6 slices bacon

1 onion, diced

2 celery stalks, chopped

1 pinch salt

1 green bell pepper, diced

1 red bell pepper, diced

3 cloves garlic, minced

1 tablespoon vegetable oil

1/3 cup flour

1 teaspoon freshly ground black pepper

1 teaspoon paprika

1/2 teaspoon dried oregano

1/4 teaspoon cayenne pepper, or to taste

3 cups cold chicken broth, divided

1 teaspoon Worcestershire sauce

8 ounces andouille sausage, sliced

2 tablespoons finely chopped green onion (white and light green parts)

2 cups shredded cooked chicken breast

1/4 cup finely chopped green onion (white and light green parts)

Salt to taste and plenty of freshly ground black pepper

Directions:

1. Cook the bacon, remove and crumble it and reserve about half the fat in the pan.

2. Over medium heat, sauté onion and celery about 5 minutes.

3. Add bell peppers and garlic and cook, another 5 minutes, until the peppers are soft.

4. Add the vegetable oil and flour, and cook, gently whisking, 5 minutes.

5. Add paprika, oregano, cayenne pepper, and plenty of black pepper, and stir to combine.

6. Add chicken broth and Worcestershire sauce, and stir the pan deeply, to remove any sticking bits. Simmer 10 minutes, stirring occasionally.

7. Add andouille sausage, chicken, and crumbled bacon, and continue cooking until andouille is cooked through.

8. Season with salt and black pepper to taste and serve topped with green onions.

CHICKEN CACCIATORE

Servings: 4 | Prep time: 10 minutes | Cooking time: 1

hour

Forget Fifty Shades — chicken cacciatore, or hunter's chicken, brings to mind Lady Chatterley's Lover. Remember the strapping gamesman who presses Lady Connie to multiple, mutual pleasures right there on the forest floor? If he's that good with his meat, he should make her this dish for dinner.

Ingredients:

8 chicken thighs, skin-on, bone-in

Salt and pepper to taste

1 cup flour

1/4 cup olive oil

2 medium onions, sliced

3 large garlic cloves, minced

2 teaspoons fresh rosemary, finely chopped

3/4 cup dry white wine

3 cans (14 1/2 ounces each) diced tomatoes, plus the juice from 1 of those cans

1 cup chicken stock

Directions:

1. Season chicken with salt and pepper and dredge in flour.

2. Heat oil in a large heavy pot over medium-high heat. Sauté the chicken, skin side first, working in batches so as not to crowd the pot. Set sautéed chicken aside.

3. Add onions, garlic, and rosemary and sauté them until the onions are translucent. Reduce heat to medium-low and add wine. Simmer about 5 minutes.

4. Stir in tomatoes, their reserved juice, the stock, and salt to taste. Return the chicken to pot and increase the heat to medium high, bringing the dish to a boil. Reduce heat to medium-low and simmer, stirring occasionally, until chicken is cooked through, 30 to 35 minutes.

5. Remove the chicken and set it aside. Increase heat and thicken the sauce. Return chicken to the pot and heat through before serving.

CHICKEN CHILE VERDE

Servings: 6 | Prep time: 30 minutes | Cooking time:

1 hour 45 minutes

If you've ever wondered about the private fantasies of New Mexico's chefs, this recipe will reveal their secret desires. Poblanos have a mild reputation, but that sometimes only barely covers a spicy surprise. Even non-spicy poblanos have a green tartness that makes this three and a half pounds of coq lip-smacking good.

Ingredients:

1 chicken, about 3 1/2 pounds

4 poblano chiles

Olive oil

1 onion, chopped

4 garlic cloves, minced

1 teaspoon cumin

1 teaspoon coriander

1 teaspoon dried oregano

2 cups chicken broth

1 cup crushed tortilla chips

Salt to taste

Leaves from 1/2 bunch fresh cilantro, chopped

Directions:

1. Bring the chicken to a boil in a large pot, reduce heat to simmer and cook until meat begins to fall from the bones. (If you throw in a couple of unpeeled carrots, broken into large pieces; half an onion; a couple of cloves of garlic and some fresh thyme, you can take the opportunity to make chicken stock.)

2. Remove the chicken from the pot, place on a cutting board and let cool to a temperature at which you can shred it with your hands.

3. Shred the meat and toss the bones.

4. Seed, core, and thinly slice the peppers.

5. In a medium saucepan over medium heat, sauté the onion and garlic in the olive oil for about 5 minutes.

6. Add the cumin, coriander, and oregano, and stir until they scent, about a minute.

7. Pour in the broth and add the crushed tortilla chips, shredded chicken, and chiles.

8. Season to taste with salt and allow to simmer for 20 minutes before serving, topped with cilantro.

CHICKEN FRICASSEE

Servings: 6 | Prep time: 20 minutes | Cooking time: 1

hour

Admit it: you secretly like your coq more than one way. Some nights you're dying for it sizzling, hot and greasy; other times you crave a slow and steamy. With fricassee, you can have it both ways! Slap that coq into hot oil to sear each side tight, then add broth (and a bunch of other goodies) and bring just to the brink of boiling. And hold it there for as long as you can, right at the edge of bubbling over, until the heat turns everything tender.

Ingredients:

1/2 cup extra-virgin olive oil

1 whole chicken, (4 pounds), cut into 10 pieces

1 green bell pepper, diced

1 red bell pepper, diced

1 onion, sliced

1 cup prepared tomato sauce

1 cup dry white wine

1 1/4 cup chicken stock

1 teaspoon cumin

1 teaspoon garlic powder

2 bay leaves

1 pound new potatoes

2 cups diced carrots

1 cup pitted green olives (no pimentos!)

1/2 cup raisins

Salt and pepper to taste

Directions:

1. Heat oil in a heavy pot and sauté chicken over medium-high until browned on all sides.

2. Add peppers, onion, chicken broth, tomato sauce, wine, chicken stock, cumin, garlic powder, and bay leaves; cook until chicken about 20 minutes before adding potatoes, carrots, olives, and raisins.

3. Continue cooking until potatoes are tender, another 20 to 25 minute.

CHICKEN POCHERO

Servings: 4 | Prep time: 15 minutes | Cooking time:

30 minutes

Question: Quien es mas macho: A coq or a banana? Answer: Doesn't' matter. In this recipe you get both!

Ingredients:

1 1/2 chicken breast, cut into bite-sized pieces

3 tablespoons vegetable oil

4 cups cubed potatoes

1 banana, cut on the bias into 1 1/2 inch pieces

1 cup prepared tomato sauce

4 garlic gloves, minced

1 small onion, quartered

1/2 teaspoon peppercorns

4 cups water

1 cup chicken stock

1 1/2 cup green beans

1 small Chinese cabbage, shredded

1 tablespoon brown sugar

2 tablespoons vegetable oil

Directions:

1.   Season chicken with salt and pepper and sauté in vegetable oil over medium heat until brown on all sides.

2.   Remove and set aside. In the same pan, sauté potatoes for five minutes, then add bananas, garlic and onion.

3.   Return the chicken to the pan and add tomato sauce, water, chicken broth and peppercorns.

4.   Simmer for about 10 minutes, then add green beans, cabbage, sugar, and salt to taste. Simmer another 10 minutes.

5.   Serve with steamed rice.

CHICKEN RED CURRY

Servings: 8 | Prep time: 25 minutes | Cooking time:
40 minutes

Not just any coq will do for this warmly spiced combo. Choose pristine white breast-meat, gently poached or simmered to its plumpest, or sautéed in hot oil to seal in its natural juices. Then bathe it in curry until it turns just-spanked pink inside, either relatively quickly, as described here, or with great anticipation and patience over a long, slow, persistent heat.

Ingredients:

2 tablespoons vegetable oil

2 onions, thinly sliced

1/3 cup red curry paste

1 medium butternut squash, peeled and cubed

8 medium carrots, cut on the bias into 2 inch pieces

2 cans unsweetened light coconut milk

2 pounds of cooked chicken breast meat, cubed or shredded

8 mini sweet peppers, sliced

Salt to taste

Directions:

1. Sauté onions in vegetable oil over medium heat until translucent. Add curry paste, squash, and carrots, and cook 3-5 minutes.

2. Add coconut milks and bring to a boil, stirring occasionally, before adding the chicken.

3. Reduce heat to a simmer and cook until vegetables are tender, 25 to 30 minutes.

4. Add peppers and simmer until they are just beginning to soften.

5. Season with salt.

CHICKEN & WHITE BEAN CHILI

Servings: 6 | Prep time: 20 minutes | Cooking time:
50 minutes

Savory chicken saturated in a creamy stew of flavors to delight any tongue. What's not to love about this very unconventional chili? If you like to heat things up a bit, slyly slip in that second serrano — or, if you're very brave, stretch yourself for a third.

Ingredients:

3 tablespoons vegetable oil

1 white onion, chopped

3 garlic cloves, minced

1 to 2 serrano chiles, seeded and minced

4 teaspoons fresh rosemary leaves, chopped

1 1/2 teaspoons ground cumin

1 teaspoon dried oregano

1/4 teaspoon cayenne pepper

Salt

1 pound ground chicken

5 cups chicken broth

1 can (15.5 ounces) cannellini beans

1 can (15 ounces) white hominy

Directions:

1. Heat oil over medium-high in a large, heavy pot and sauté onion for about 10 minutes.

2. Add garlic, chiles, rosemary, cumin, oregano, and cayenne and sauté them until they scent, about 2 minutes.

3. Season to taste with salt. Add chicken and cook, breaking up meat, about 10 minutes. Add broth, beans, and hominy and bring the chili to a boil. Reduce heat, and simmer 20-25 minutes.

4. Serve with warmed corn tortillas.

GRANDMOTHER'S CHICKEN MATZO BALL SOUP

Servings: 6 | Prep time: 20 minutes, plus 2-4 hours

to chill | Cooking time: 1 hour

A book about coq is not the place to talk about your grandmother, so that's exactly what we'll do! In this case, imagine ol' Granny rolling a pair of balls gently between her hands...Matzo balls, that is.

Ingredients:

3 eggs

3 tablespoons vegetable oil, or, better yet, chicken fat

1 1/2 teaspoons salt

3/4 cup plus 2 tablespoons matzo meal

10 cups chicken broth

3 carrots, sliced into rounds

Fresh dill, minced

Directions:

1. Whisk together eggs and chicken fat until thoroughly combined, then add 1/2 cup water and salt.

2. Add matzo meal, and stir until combined. Cover the batter and refrigerate it 2-4 hours, until firm.

3. Line a baking sheet with parchment.

4. In a large wide saucepan, bring chicken stock to a boil, then reduce to a simmer.

5. Using your hands, form the batter into balls of about 1 1/2 inches wide, but don't press them too hard. Set the balls aside as you work.

6. Using a spoon or ladle, lower the matzo balls into the simmering stock. When all the balls are in the soup, cover the pot and simmer for 10 minutes before adding carrots.

7. Simmer for another 20-25 minutes. A matzo ball is ready when, removed from the soup and cut in half, it is uniform in color inside, not darker in the center. Serve the soup sprinkled with dill.

GREEN COCONUT CHICKEN

Servings: 4 | Prep time: 30 minutes | Cooking time:

30 minutes

The assertive lash of tangy lime cooled by creamy coconut reminiscent of sexy Thai beaches. Spread it over a bed of steamed rice, letting the juices saturate each plain white grain so they burst with flavor.

Ingredients:

1 tablespoon cornstarch

1 can (14.5 ounces) chicken broth

2 tablespoons vegetable oil

2 green bell peppers, chopped

1 medium onion (1/2 inch thick), halved and sliced

1 to 2 tablespoons Thai green curry paste

4 cooked boneless, skinless chicken breasts, cut into 1-inch pieces

1 can (14.5 ounces) coconut milk

1 cup fresh basil leaves

2 tablespoons fresh lime juice

Salt to taste

Directions:

1.   In a large skillet over medium, heat the oil and sauté bell peppers and onion, 5 to 7 minutes.

2.   Add curry paste and cook, stirring and scraping bottom of skillet, 3 to 4 minutes.

3.   Whisk cornstarch with 2 to 3 tablespoons chicken broth in a small bowl and add it to the vegetables along with the chicken, coconut milk, and the rest of the chicken broth.

4.   Simmer until chicken is warmed through and vegetables are cooked to your liking. Add the basil and lime juice, stirring to combine them well.

5.   Season to taste with salt. Serve with steamed rice.

UGANDAN CHICKEN IN PEANUT SAUCE

Servings: 6 | Prep time: 20 minutes | Cooking time: 90 minutes

Are there pleasures you're drawn to if maybe just a little afraid of? Intense, dark and rich delights that burn your senses while still leaving a lingering sweetness you can't forget? Add this recipe to the list. The combination of peanut butter and cayenne is hot and creamy!

Ingredients:

2 1/2 pounds chicken thighs, skin-on and bone-in

3 tablespoons vegetable oil

1 large yellow or white onion, sliced

2 tablespoons mince ginger

8 garlic cloves, crushed

2 large sweet potatoes, peeled and cut into chunks

1 15-ounce can of crushed tomatoes 1 quart chicken stock 1 cup smooth, unsweetened peanut butter

1 cup roasted peanuts

1 tablespoon ground coriander

1 teaspoon cayenne, or to taste

Salt and black pepper

1/4 to 1/2 cup of chopped cilantro

Directions:

1. Salt the chicken thoroughly In a large soup pot set over medium-high heat, heat the oil and sauté the chicken until brown on all sides. Work in batches if you need to, and set aside chicken pieces as they are cooked.

2. Sauté the onions in the same pan for 3-4 minutes, scraping up the browned bits. Add the ginger and garlic and sauté another couple of minutes, then add the sweet potatoes and toss thoroughly to combine.

3. Return the cooked chicken to the pan and add the chicken broth, crushed tomatoes, peanut butter, peanuts, coriander and cayenne. Bring to a simmer and taste for salt. Simmer gently for 90 minutes, stirring occasionally, until the chicken falls off the bone.

4. Remove the chicken pieces and discard the bones. When the chicken has cooled enough to touch, remove the skin and shred the chicken; return it to the pot.

5. Serve over steamed rice.

Roleplaying

TARTS, PIES AND CASSEROLES

Chicken & Asparagus Pie

Servings: 6 | Prep time: 30 minutes | Cooking time: 35 minutes

And you thought asparagus was sexy just because of its shape: it's an aphrodisiac! That's because it's full of folic (no, not phallic — what a filthy mind you have) acid, which practically guarantees orgasms.

Ingredients:

3 tablespoons butter

1/4 cup chopped onion

2 tablespoons flour

1 cup half-and-half

Salt and pepper to taste

2 cups cubed chicken

1 cup asparagus tips

1/2 cup sliced fresh mushrooms

3 tablespoons dry white wine

1 can refrigerated crescent rolls

Directions:

1. Heat oven to 350°F.

2. Melt butter over medium heat in a large sauce pan. Sauté onion for 5 minutes.

Whisk in flour; and cook for another 5 minutes or so.

3. Gradually add half-and-half, then salt and pepper to taste. Heat to boiling, stirring constantly. Remove from heat and add the chicken, asparagus, mushrooms and wine.

4. Separate dough into 8 triangles and flatten them into an ungreased 9-inch pie plate with the pointy ends at the rim of the plate.

5. Fill the crust with the chicken mixture and fold in the tips of rolls to cover the filling.

6. Bake 25 to 30 minutes.

CHICKEN & BUTTERNUT SQUASH COTTAGE PIE

Servings: 6 | Prep time: 30 minutes | Cooking time: 45 minutes

Naughty coq lovers sometimes have to eat humble pie. Here's a perfect recipe for such a remedial occasion — traditional cottage pie made up-to-date with tender butternut squash.

Ingredients:

---

3 tablespoons melted butter

1 yellow onion, diced medium

2 large carrots, sliced

Salt and pepper to taste

2 tablespoons tomato paste

1 pound ground chicken

2 teaspoons fresh thyme

1 cup chicken broth

2 tablespoons flour

3/4 cup frozen peas

1 large russet potato (3/4 pound), very thinly sliced

Directions:

1. Preheat oven to 400 degrees.

2. Heat 1 tablespoon butter over medium heat in a large. Add onion and carrots and sauté 5 minutes. Add tomato paste, then chicken, and cook, another 3 minutes, breaking up ground chicken.

3. Increase heat and add chicken broth and thyme. Let chicken come to a boil and cook, stirring frequently, 5 minutes. Add the flour and whisk to combine.

4. Add 1 cup water and bring to a brief boil again. Stir in peas and season with salt and pepper.

5. Pour into a 2-quart baking dish. Top with potato slices.

6. Season the top with salt and pepper and drizzle it with melted butter. Bake 40 minutes, watching to see that the potatoes don't get too brown. Let cool 10 minutes before serving.

CHICKEN QUICHE

Servings: 6 | Prep time: 15 minutes | Cooking time:

1 hour

What's the old saying, "real men don't eat quiche?" Here's a recipe for coq-and-broc to prove that wrong.

Ingredients:

2 tablespoons butter

1 onion, diced

3 cloves garlic, minced

Salt and pepper to taste

2 cups cooked chicken, cut in bite-size pieces or shredded

2 cups cooked broccoli florets, cut in bite-size pieces

1 1/2 cups shredded sharp cheddar cheese

1/4 cup grated Parmesan cheese

1 pie crust

4 eggs

3/4 cup heavy cream

3/4 cup milk

Directions:

1. Preheat oven to 350 degrees.

2. Sauté the onion and garlic in butter until tender and season to taste with salt and pepper.

3. Mix the chicken, broccoli, both cheeses and onion and garlic together with your hands or a wooden spoon, in a large bowl.

4. Line a 9-inch dish pie dish with the pie crust and fill it with the chicken mixture.

5. Whisk the eggs, heavy cream and milk and pour them into the pie crust. Cover the edges of the crust with foil.

6. Bake for 45 minutes, remove the foil, and bake another 10 minutes, until the center is set. Allow to set 10 minutes before serving.

Korean Chicken & Cheese Buldak

Servings: 6 | Prep time: 10 minutes | Cooking time:

25 minutes

Get ready to spice up dinner with half a cup of hot pepper flakes and paste. You have to be careful what sensitive body parts you touch when you've handled all that spiciness, but apparently it's just fine to rub it all over your coq.

Ingredients:

½ cup hot pepper flakes

2 to 3 tablespoons Korean hot pepper paste

1 tablespoon soy sauce

3 tablespoons vegetable oil, divided

½ teaspoon ground black pepper

⅓ cup rice syrup or honey

6 garlic cloves, minced

2 teaspoons ginger, minced

¼ cup water

2 pounds of cooked chicken breast, cubed

1 pound mozzarella cheese, cubed

1 green onion, chopped

Directions:

1. Preheat the oven broiler.

2. Combine hot pepper flakes, hot pepper paste, soy sauce, 2 tablespoons vegetable oil, black pepper, rice syrup or honey, garlic, ginger and water in a bowl. Add the chicken and blend well.

3. Heat the remaining vegetable oil in a large skillet and sauté the marinated chicken. Add the spice mixture, cover and cook over medium heat for 10 minutes.

4. Reduce the heat and simmer another 10 minutes.

5. When the chicken is cooked, sprinkle the top with cheese and place the pan under the broiler until the cheese is brown.

Moroccan-Style Bastilla

Servings: 8 | Prep time: 45 minutes | Cooking time:
1 hour

Here's a sexy recipe dominated by a ménage a trois of flavors — chicken, a heady spice mix, and melt-in-your-mouth phyllo dough. And you get to make it slick and luscious with two whole sticks of butter!

Ingredients:

2 tablespoons olive oil, divided

3 chicken breasts

1 onion, chopped

3 garlic cloves, minced

1 teaspoon fresh ginger, peeled and finely chopped

2 teaspoons cinnamon

1 teaspoon cumin

1 teaspoon coriander

1/2 teaspoon ground red pepper

1/2 teaspoon turmeric

1/4 teaspoon saffron powder

1 cup chicken broth

2 tablespoons cilantro, torn

1 tablespoon fresh parsley leaves, chopped

7 eggs, lightly beaten

1 teaspoon salt

1/2 teaspoon ground black pepper

1 lb. phyllo dough

1 cup butter (2 sticks)

Topping for Phyllo Leaves:

1/2 cup confectioners' sugar (optional)

1 teaspoon ground cinnamon (optional)

Topping for Filling:

1 1/2 cups blanched almonds, slivered or chopped

2 tablespoons sugar

2 teaspoons ground cinnamon

Directions:

1. Heat 1 tablespoon olive oil over medium-high heat in large skillet. Add chicken breasts and sauté until golden brown on all sides, about 5 minutes. Remove chicken from skillet and set aside.

2. In same skillet, sauté onions, garlic, ginger, in the remaining 1 tablespoon oil.

3. Stir in cinnamon, cumin, coriander, red pepper, turmeric, and saffron. Reduce to low and cook, stirring, another 5 minutes.

4. Add broth, cilantro, and parsley to skillet with onion mixture and increase the heat to high. Heat to boiling, stirring regularly. Return chicken to skillet, cover and reduce heat to low, simmering until chicken is tender, 25 minutes.

5. Remove chicken and set aside to cool. Continue to cook what's left in the skillet covered, until almost dry, about 15 minutes.

6. Add eggs, cook until soft curds form, about 3 minutes, and season with salt and pepper. Remove skillet from the heat.

7. When chicken is cool enough to handle, remove and discard skin and bones and shred the chicken.

Topping:

1. In food processor, pulse the almonds with sugar and cinnamon until coarsely ground.

To Assemble Bastilla:

1. Phyllo dries very quickly, so always keep any exposed leaves covered with a damp towel.

2. Preheat oven to 350 degrees and brush 2 12-inch pizza or other round pans with melted butter.

3. Place 1 leaf of Phyllo on pan, letting the edges hang over the rim. Brush that leaf with butter, stack another leaf and butter it,

and continue until you have a stack of 12 leaves.

4. At the center of the stack, spread half the topping, half the onion-egg mixture, and all the shredded chicken strips. Top that with the second half of the onion-egg mixture, and the remaining topping.

5. Fold the edges of the phyllo leaves over top of the bastilla and brush with butter.

6. Now you'll build another stack of 12 butter Phyllo leaves on top of the work you've already completed. This time, tuck in overhanging phyllo as you work, making a neat side. Brush the sides with melted butter.

7. Bake bastilla in the preheated oven for 20 minutes or until golden.

8. Remove the bastilla, and turn it completely upside down by placing the second buttered pan on top of the bastille and flipping it. Return the bastilla to the oven and bake 20 minutes longer or until crisp and golden.

9. Top with confectioners' sugar and ground cinnamon.

White Lasagna

Servings: 12 | Prep time: 25 minutes | Cooking time:

50 minutes

When ready, this sexy lasagna will be creaming for you to fork it.

Ingredients:

9 lasagna noodles

1/2 cup butter

1 onion, chopped

1 clove garlic, minced

1/2 cup flour

Salt to taste

2 cups chicken broth

1 1/2 cups milk

4 cups shredded mozzarella cheese, divided

1 cup grated Parmesan cheese, divided

1 teaspoon dried basil

1 teaspoon dried oregano

2 cups ricotta cheese

2 cups cubed, cooked chicken meat

2 (10 ounce) packages frozen chopped spinach, thawed and drained

1 tablespoon chopped fresh parsley

1/4 cup grated Parmesan cheese

Salt and pepper to taste

Directions:

1. Preheat oven to 350 degrees.

2. Cook the lasagna according to package directions; drain it and set aside.

3. In a large saucepan over medium heat sauté the onion and garlic in the butter.

4. Whisk in the flour and cook, stirring, for 2 minutes. Add broth and milk, and to a low boil, stirring constantly, for 1 minute.

5. Add 2 cups mozzarella and 1/4 cup Parmesan cheese. Add basil, oregano, and season with salt and pepper. Remove from heat.

6. Spoon 1/3 of the sauce mixture into a 9x13 inch baking dish. Top that layer with 3 lasagna noodles, then the ricotta, and the chicken. Add another layer of noodles, topping it with sauce, spinach, mozzarella and 1 cup of parmesan. Add the next layer of noodles on top of that, top with sauce and sprinkle on the final quarter cup of parmesan.

7. Bake 35 to 40 minutes.

Taming An Unruly Coq

TIPS AND TOOLS OF THE TRADE

You might not realize it, but even the most vanilla kitchen has a majority of the proper instruments of coq-taming. Most of us have been playing with coq all our lives, making it into all sorts of juicy concoctions with just the tools we have at hand: a sharp knife, a sauce pan and a roasting pan, barbecue tools and maybe a baster. A couple of other things that might come in handy include:

A Meat Thermometer

We believe in cooking chicken to an internal 160 degrees. That's not too dry, not too slimy. Plus, it's what the government recommends to prevent food poisoning.

Kitchen Twine

The debate about trussing continues. Some of our friends are for, some of our friends are against it, and we're with our friends. If you choose to truss, get yourself some decent kitchen twine. It won't burn, and it's easy to handle with greasy fingers.

Vertical Roaster

This is the tool to get if you're serious about roasting whole birds on the grill. It's an upgrade from the cooking-hacking method of balancing the chicken on a beer can on the grill. It holds the chicken upright on the grill, with a reservoir for holding liquids to keep the chicken moist.

Meat Injector

These rather clinical looking implements are for shooting liquid marinades and flavors under the chicken's skin before cooking. A great way to make chicken moist and flavorful without taking time to brine or marinate.

Tenderizer

You can flatten boneless chicken breasts adequately with just about anything heavy and sturdy— a small frying pan will do the job. But a real meat tenderizer provides more control and precision.

Most of them have a spiked side that pierces the flesh to soften it and allow more flavor to penetrate, and a smooth side for more gentle banging.

A Few Insider Tips To Make Coq-Ery

Use a Thermometer

Always use a thermometer to know when your chicken is cooked, rather than cutting into the meat. Chicken is cooked when it's 160 degrees Fahrenheit. Forget about all those directions about how loosely a leg wiggles, or the color of the juices when you pierce the thigh. Just get the thermometer.

Brine all the time!

Put your chicken in brine in the morning and you'll have juicy chicken at night no matter the recipe. What's the difference between a brine and a marinade? Marinades add flavor.

The main purpose of a brine is to produce meat that is super moist. You can add flavor to a brine (more on that in a second), but its main ingredients are water and salt. How much brine you'll need is based on how much chicken you're cooking, but a standard ratio is one quart of water and 1/4 cup of salt. One to six hours in that will give you really moist chicken. For a restaurant-delicious flavor that goes with any chicken preparation you can think of, add a 1/4 cup of sugar to your brine.

And yes, you can add spices and other flavors to your brine. Garlic, peppercorns, herbs — pretty much any flavor you'd add to a marinade.

QUICKIE BRINE

Ingredients:

3 cups hot water

1/4 cup salt

1/4 cup sugar

1-2 cups ice

Directions:

1. In a large bowl, combine water, salt, and sugar and stir till dissolved. Add the ice and stir until that's dissolved too.

2. Let chicken soak in this mixture in the refrigerator either covered in a bowl, or in a zipper-lock bag, for 1-6 hours, or heck, overnight if you feel like it. This is one recipe you can't mess up.

Made in United States
Orlando, FL
12 December 2024